Sandra LaMorgese, PhD

5 STEPS For Better Communication, Sex and Happiness

(Did I Mention Better Sex?)

Editing by Jessica Bowen
jessicajbowen.com

Interior and Cover Design by EdgePlay Publication
Published by EdgePlay Publishing

ISBN-10: 0-9862639-3-1
ISBN-13: 978-0-9862639-3-4

EdgePlay

PUBLISHING

Sandra LaMorgese PhD

5 STEPS For Better Communication, Sex and Happiness
(Did I Mention Better Sex?)

EdgePlay

PUBLISHING

Dedication:

*To my communication Masters
who taught me to take risks and believe
in the power of my
individual voice.*

"The basic building block of good communications is the feeling that every human being is unique and of value."

—Unkown

Contents

CHAPTER 1

Introduction

Everyone wants to know the secrets to a good, healthy, exciting relationship. We swim through an endless stream of magazine articles, blog posts, books, and advice from friends and family, desperately hoping that we'll find the secret to finding, growing, and sustaining a truly loving relationship. For many of us, this quest takes up a huge amount of our thoughts and energy, especially if we start the journey with a trail of painful, failed relationships behind us.

In this book, though, I have the answer we've all been searching for: the key that can unlock your potential to become a more loving partner, a more self-aware and confident person, and a more sexually invigorated and satisfied lover. Does it sound too good to be true? Are you ready to be enlightened? Here it is:

The secret to having a great relationship—the foundation, the key, the map that leads you to a chest of priceless buried treasure—is communication.

I know, I know. I'm pretty sure I just heard you groan out loud. You've heard this a thousand times already, and besides, communicating well with a partner is really f-ing hard. I can hear your frustration all the way from my apartment, where I'm daring to write the same advice that has been said before for years, decades, and centuries. Here's where this book is different though—I'm not going to leave you hanging. You've had enough people tell you that all you need to do is "Tell him how you really feel" or "Just be honest and tell her what you really want." Everyone knows that, somehow, communication is essential to a successful relationship, but very few people can tell you where those good communication skills are supposed to come from. They don't magically appear, that's for sure. Strong communication is a skill, like rock climbing or learning a new language, and skills take practice. In this book, I will share a few of the strategies that science and life experience have taught me about how to communicate in a way that is consistent, authentic, and has the power to transform your entire life.

First of all, we should explore why communicating in relationships (or when exploring a potential relationship) can be so difficult. We are not born with highly developed communication skills, and if we don't grow up in a family of open communicators it can be an uphill battle to learn how to communicate well, and many are left to develop the skill on their own.

When humans started communicating 2 million years ago I'm sure it sounded something like "Ugh." And believe me, personal experience has taught me that interpersonal communication in the 21st century hasn't developed much past the "ugh" stage for lots of us.

As a female, I was taught to be polite, not raise my voice (hell, I wasn't allowed to have a voice), and to act as the peace-maker; in other words, to avoid making waves at all cost. Basically this meant that for the first 35 years of my life I could not be fully present in any of my personal relationships. I constantly thought about what I needed and wanted, but expressing it was out of the question. It was like having a lock on my inner voice and no key to access it. My self-esteem was tragically lowered as a result of my ongoing inability to speak the truth as I felt it and I continually beat myself up for not having the courage to stand up for my needs. It took earning a B.A. in communication studies and years of practice before I felt capable of simply articulating what I thought and felt. Not as easy as it sounds!

As if that weren't enough, we live in a society that has trained us to be terrible listeners. Between TV, social media, email, cell phones, and the constant flood of updates we receive about things happening to other people in other places, many of us have lost the art of being present. You need to be present to be an effective listener. Texting, watching TV, staring out the window while you're partner is speaking to you is NOT the way to go, but many of us have a tough time quieting our minds long enough to let another person speak their mind and really pay attention to what they're saying and who they are right in the moment. But taking the time to listen without inserting your own responses may allow you to hear things you've never heard before.

The final nail in our communication coffin is that we have become just as bad at listening to ourselves as we are at listening to others. Before you can ever expect to tune in to what your partner has to say, you need to start listening to the voice that resides inside you. Does it encourage you? Assure you that you are confident, kind, and loving to yourself and others? Or does it constantly beat you up with self-doubt, denial, criticism, and self-hatred? One of the ways to become better at listening to others is to become better at listening to ourselves through self-reflection and observation. One of my favorite tricks to overcome self-doubt and negative thoughts is to ask myself, "Who taught me that?" Was it my mother, my father, a teacher, an ex? Once I identify the outside influence, I can usually let it go.

When we can effectively listen to our authentic self, or "inner soul," and not the mind chatter we generally allow to run our thoughts, we can incorporate those skills in listening to others as well: we can listen, reflect, and then respond. If we don't know how to separate our own inner voice from the hundreds of voices that have tried to tell us what to do and how to feel for our whole lives, though, we will have a pretty hazy idea of what our true desires are. If you don't know what makes you you, what makes you happy, and what you want apart from all of those outside voices, you'll have a hard time connecting authentically with a partner. The sooner we can learn to listen to that truthful inner voice, the better, because it gets infinitely harder to really listen to that voice once you're already in a committed relationship.

With the odds stacked against us like this, is it any wonder that many of us are baffled or frustrated when it comes to providing a safe, caring environment where we can communicate our own needs and listen to our partner's needs? It's true: all of these communication obstacles take time and practice to overcome and the process involves unlearning a lot of bad habits, but the end result is a beautiful gift of giving and receiving that will spill over into all areas of your life and is truly worth the hard work it takes to achieve.

This book is designed to help you to understand that communication is a skillful dance between partners that can be learned. Sometimes the song will play forever and sometimes for only a little while, but regardless of how long you dance with any one person, every time you practice, you'll become a little more graceful and a little more confident. It's all about keeping your dancing shoes on so that you're ready to move whenever you feel the urge.

CHAPTER 2

The Five Steps of a Sexy, Loving Relationship

In 1983, psychologist George Levinger, a psychology professor at the University of Massachusetts at Amherst, published one of the leading models of the relationship growth. According to Levinger, the stages of the relationship process are as follows:

1. **Acquaintance.** Becoming acquainted depends on previous relationships, physical proximity, first impressions, and a variety of other factors. If two people begin to like each other, continued interactions may lead to the next stage, but the stage of acquaintance can continue indefinitely.

2. **Buildup.** During this stage, people begin to trust and care about each other. The need for

compatibility and such filtering agents as common background and goals will influence whether or not the interaction will continue.

3. **Continuation**. This stage follows a "mutual commitment" to a long-term friendship, romantic relationship, or marriage. It is generally a long, relatively stable period. Nevertheless, continued growth and development will occur during this time. Mutual trust is important for sustaining the relationship.

4. **Deterioration**. Not all relationships deteriorate, but those that do tend to show signs of trouble. Boredom, resentment, and dissatisfaction may occur, and individuals may communicate less and avoid self-disclosure. Loss of trust and betrayals may take place as the downward spiral continues.

5. **Termination**. This final stage marks the end of the relationship, either by death in the case of a healthy relationship, or by separation.

Our sexual and romantic relationships don't necessarily always follow this healthy progression as outlined by Levinger. Sometimes we jump directly from acquaintance to continuation, forgetting how important the trust and caring of the buildup stage is.

And then just when we thought things were moving along nicely, termination comes along! We wonder what went wrong when it's already over. Every step is important, and each comes with its own set of nuances. Understanding each phase and how the overall progression works together is the first step toward using your knowledge to develop better self-awareness and better relationship skills.

CHAPTER 3

Step One:
The Acquaintance Phase

The first encounter with a new person can amount to something as simple as a "hello." Greetings are usually verbal, but can be nothing more than a nonverbal cue or the combination of a verbal and nonverbal cue simultaneously. You might say "hi," wave your hand, or offer a handshake as you say, "Hello, it's nice to meet you." A great way to connect nonverbally is to offer a smile, but either way it's that simple: a smile, a word and/or a wave and you are now engaged. If you do not get a verbal or nonverbal cue in return that suggests that the individual wants to continue the interaction, the connection is likely over. In that case, move on. No harm done. However, if the connection continues as you'd like or planned, keep in mind you are still in the acquaintance phase.

It's easy to feel nervous or anxious about what to say to the new hottie who's walking your way. Who doesn't clam up or ramble on during the first greeting from time to time? But think about it: This is their first encounter too, and I suspect they're shaking in their shoes. So, when the hottie asks, "How ya doin'?" (this one's from New Jersey), don't panic. Instead, try to mirror the tone and content of the greeting you've received. For example: "How are you?" might encourage you to say, "I'm fine, how are you?" If at that point you wish to open more of a conversation, find something in common to talk about. Talk about what you're doing at that particular moment. Don't be the person who answers "How are you?" with a 15-minute tirade about every little detail of their day. You know, the next-door neighbor (when you're climbing into your car and late for work) or the coworker (when you're on your way to an important meeting). I recently went to pay for something at my local drugstore and greeted the woman behind the cash register with "Hey, how are you?" Unfortunately, the cashier took this as a signal to tell me every tragic episode that she had had the misfortune to endure over the past year. Not an appropriate response to an informal greeting, especially one from a stranger!

The important thing is to keep the message positive and allow—and encourage—the conversation to continue to flow. Here are a few possible typical situations:

- **You're at a concert and the hottie sits next to you.** "Wow," (you say after a brief nod or "hi") "I've had these tickets for a month. I've really been looking forward to seeing these guys. Have you ever heard them live before?"

- **You're getting a drink at the water cooler at work.** "I love this 15-minute break mid-morning —it totally energizes me. ...I think I've seen you around the office, right? Which department do you work in?"

- **Running/walking for a charity event.** "What a great turnout today! I'm so excited about running this race."

I hope you didn't forget to smile right off the bat, too! Okay, so now let's say things are moving along nicely, and the conversation stays buoyant. It's time to ask yourself what your goals are, or your reasons for perpetuating the conversation. For the most part, they will involve wanting to influence, learn, assist, amuse, relate, or any other number of possibilities. Even all of the above. In addition, there is really no timeframe on how long an acquaintance stage might last. It all depends on the situation. Just remember that a true conversation is between two (or more) people who converse back and forth. A good rule of thumb is to listen twice as much as you speak. The only way you're going to learn about another person is to listen to them.

According to Webster's online dictionary, one definition for acquaintance is "a person whom one knows, but who is not a particularly close friend, a casual acquaintance." In other words, an "acquaintance" is someone you know, who exists on the same planet as you do. You might know nothing about this person. Not how he drinks his coffee, if she has brothers or sisters, or if they have a secret talent for playing the tuba...in other words, you probably have no intimate details about this person whatsoever!

Having no intimate details does not, however, mean that there is a lack of sexual energy. In fact, a lack of knowledge can encourage the sexual attraction, which may be impossible to deny or ignore. For now, feel secure in knowing that those sexual feelings are real, and that both your vibrations are blending perfectly. Enjoy your sexuality in this exciting early phase; don't deny it. It's up to you to decide how to act on these physical feelings. You might want to go for it and have a one-night stand of safe sex. Whatever you decide, the point is to have fun.

I realized early on how important honest communication was in my quest for sexual freedom and empowerment. My skills were put to the test when I saw Rob's profile on line, and I decided to give him a wink despite the 14-year age difference between us. What the hell, he was my type. Rob got back to me within 30 minutes and asked, "Okay, you're 53 and I'm 39. Where are you expecting this relationship to go?" Hmm... I sat behind my keyboard wondering how to handle this suddenly delicate conversation. "Now, be honest," he continued. "Because you might get exactly what you're looking for. I have no problem being with an older woman when she's as hot as you are."

I thought about it nervously for a minute, and then responded. "Well, I thought if we met and there was an attraction between us, we'd have an incredible sexual relationship." Five minutes later Rob wrote back. "Hello, naughty sexy Sandra..." It was so liberating to be completely honest in my communication with this man, and I loved how he put it right on the table and asked me to share want I wanted. No games.

With that said—and I don't care if he claims he eats pussy like a rock star—if your intentions are to build an intimate, loving, trusting relationship it might be a better idea to hold off on the sexual contact, at least for a time. Also, if you're unsure whether you feel comfortable enough to have an open conversation about intentions prior to any physical contact, it could be too soon in your relationship to go there. Nobody likes to be in the position of wondering if their one-night stand will call the next day. If this is you after your first night of sex with a new partner, it's a sure sign that you've skipped too far ahead in the stages, with some not so great side-effects. Temporary flings can be healthy and fun, but remember that you have to be prepared well in advance to accept the encounter for what it is and not place your hopes and dreams on continuing the relationship. In other words, you have to be confident that you can walk away afterwards with your happiness and confidence intact.

And, this early on, if at any point you feel that your hottie is not right for you after all or you realize that you want different things from the relationship, just end the interaction! That's the beauty of the acquaintance stage. If things aren't going well during your first few interactions, there are several ways to escape cleanly.

Like the greeting or opening of each conversation, effective closings can be handled with a verbal cue, a nonverbal cue, or both. Personally, I prefer the nonverbal cue followed by a verbal cue when you're ready to complete your interaction and when it's face-to-face. You'd be surprised how fast people get it, and realize you mean it—that the conversation is now over. Here are a few of my favorite ways to bring a conversation to a successful close:

- **Be direct**. Close your book..."It's been nice chatting, but I have to go."

- **Rehash the conversation to facilitate your exit.** Finish your drink... "Okay...so, now I know you frequent this club on Thursday nights, so, um... take care...I'll see you later."

• **Make a reference to talking again in the future.** Stand up..."So, let's exchange numbers. Maybe we can get together after the holidays." (Maybe or maybe not)

• **Express that you enjoyed yourself.** A handshake or a kiss, depending on how you feel, while saying, "Well, it was really nice meeting you." (Absolutely, if you feel that way)

Now that wasn't so bad, right? You had your first encounter with the hottie. Possibly you decided to end the dance right then and there. However, if the two of you had a few sparks fly you might have decided to give him a second thought.

All of this comes with an important side note: as a rule, society typically expects men to be more assertive in their communications than women. For that reason many women hang in there until the man decides it's time to end the conversation or interaction. Hear me when I say that it does not need to happen this way. Men, you should never feel pressure to direct the entire conversation. Some men aren't forward, dominant types, and that's just fine! Women, don't feel like you need to wait for cues from him in the conversation. If it feels right, take the initiative to start or end the conversation! Male or female, we need to put ourselves in control of our needs and wants, and when we do this successfully, it feels extremely empowering and freeing. Start observing yourself in your interactions: How often do you make the choice to open or close the exchange, and do you typically lead or follow during the exchange? Does this feel natural to you? Does it feel natural between you and the person you're talking to? Just remember that this is not an exact science, but if you follow your instincts and act in a way that feels natural and fits with your personality and feelings, you can't go wrong.

So, now what? You've met the person you're interested in, and things seem to be going well. You've chatted a couple times, you know their name and maybe a few of their interests, and since you've been paying close attention to communication lately, you also have a pretty good sense of their communication style. You think there's a chance that the two of you could be a good match, and you want to keep building on the mutual interest and attraction. Congratulations! You've reached the building stage!

CHAPTER 4

Step Two: The BuildUp Stage

Wasn't it Chris Rock who said: "We don't show up for the first date, we send our representative"? We naturally want to make a great first impression, so early in the dating process, we want to show off our best side. This is great, as long as it doesn't go too far and lead us to start faking who we really are. Take my word for it, this never works well for the long haul. Be brave! You know who you are; now let your date know what really matters to you. Allow your authentic self to shine through. It will only take a moment for them to pick up on any pretense—and when they do, you can forget about developing trust. You've only started getting to know each other, so feel free to show more than one side of yourself. We are not one-dimensional creatures; first dates would be pretty boring if we were!

Sharing your dreams and passions is a fantastic way to get to know one other. OMG, don't you just love listening to someone who's passionate about what they do every day?! You can feel the energy crackling in the air around them. This energy creates a positive atmosphere for conversation and creates a perfect environment for developing trust, intimacy, and passion. By sharing a deeper part of ourselves, we are showing that we are confident enough to trust another person with our feelings, hopes, and dreams for the future as well.

Remember the conversational mirroring you did earlier, when you'd only just met? It still works just as well! Try mirroring the other person's tone and energy (while still being honest and authentic). The next thing you know, they'll be sharing their feelings, hopes, and dreams for the future with you too. If this mirroring feels easy and natural, that's an excellent early sign that you have a good dynamic.

Of course, it would be great if all this happened on the first date, but the reality is that sometimes building intimacy and trust using honest communication can happen quickly, but sometimes it takes some time. Don't get discouraged if it isn't perfect right away, and just keep practicing your positive tone, body language, and authenticity.

We all come from different psychological and emotional places. Some of us trust easily, but for others it can be a struggle to let ourselves go enough to trust someone else with our feelings. At this stage of the relationship there's a double-edged sword when it comes to intimacy. We want to trust someone enough to believe that they won't hurt us, but that can't happen when we're so busy being self-protective to avoid getting hurt! Naturally this means we may often find it difficult to open up to a more intimate connection.

Remember, though, this is only the buildup stage, so it's okay to take baby steps if you're having trust issues. It can help to think of it in this way: Try risking only as much of your emotional self as you believe the potential level of hurt might be that you could experience if the relationship doesn't work out. In other words, ask yourself if you're willing to pay the "consequences" and check in regularly with yourself to know how much you're risking. For example, as we mentioned earlier, if you have sex too early in the relationship and you don't hear from the other person again—and you never made the effort to reach out to them afterwards—will you be devastated, cool with it, or somewhere in between the two? Paying attention to this balance will help you avoid being blindsided with hurt feelings if, for whatever reason, things don't work out.

After Gary and I had "in-person sex" for the first time I didn't hear from him. After a week, I decided to take matters into my own hands by texting him. I mean, WTF, right? We'd communicated almost every day for months, and then after sex all communication stopped! I typed out, "Hey baby, can I ask you something?" After about a minute Gary responded. "What's up?" I stayed calm. "Why have you been acting like such an asshole for the past week?"

Gary's response? "Whoa, you've been acting different all week, too!" And he was right. I wasn't devastated by our sudden distance, but neither was I cool with the way we hadn't communicated at all after our sexual encounter. I was somewhere in between and confused, and speculating about how he was feeling certainly didn't help. Can you just imagine the energy I wasted for a whole week trying to figure out why the communication between us had suddenly ceased? Instead, I should have just picked up the phone and texted him the day after, or at least earlier in the week. Clearly, Gary and I were having intimacy and trust issues after sex. The best thing we could have done would have been to talk about how we were feeling instead of guessing at what the other was feeling and thinking—and getting it wrong.

During this phase, you start to learn about who the other person really is based on their actions, and not just their words. Say your date shows up an hour late without a good reason and you're pissed. In this case, firmly express that you will not tolerate waiting and that it's important to you that people respect your time. We all need boundaries and need to set limits for what we will and will not tolerate. If your date does cross one of your boundaries, be firm about telling them how you truly feel--chances are, it won't go away on its own, and the sooner you lay out your priorities, the sooner you'll be able to figure out if you're a good match together. Too many of us are under the impression that we need to be "nice" all the time or our romantic interests won't like us. I say, too fucking bad if they don't! Be considerate, but if the other person can't handle your real opinions and feelings, they're not worth keeping around anyway. You might be surprised though--if you're honest and up front, they might actually like you even more because self-respect is very sexy. When your date realizes how much you respect yourself, chances are they will conclude that you are also respectful of others. Would you want to date a doormat? By showing who you are up front you and your partner(s) will build trust and intimacy.

The building stage is where couples often hit a turning point in the relationship. You're closer than you were during the acquaintance stage, and you've started to see how they act, around you and around other people. You start practicing communication and learning how your individual styles do or don't mesh. This time is an amazing opportunity to reassess the nature of the interaction. Are things working well enough to continue seeing each other? Have you noticed any red flags? Do you have frequent misunderstandings, or has everything been smooth sailing so far? Think about these things on your own, and if it feels right, talk with the other person about them too. Once again, the key is honesty! If you're trying to build a strong relationship of trust, you can't waste any time (least of all this precious trust-building time at the beginning) pretending to be someone you're not or to want things that you don't.

Think of the building stage as a series of stops on a spiral staircase that you're climbing together. You start off at the bottom of the stairs, gazing into each other eyes, totally optimistic, holding each other's hand with one hand, holding their bootie with the other. After a little bit of climbing, though, the stairs will start to feel steeper and more exhausting. When this happens, it's a good time to sit down on a step together and decide if it's worth continuing the climb as a pair. If not, slide right down the banister crying "whoopee!" all the way. If you do decide you want to move forward, muster your strength and keep climbing (bootie still in hand). Eventually you'll reach a landing on the staircase that leads to a nice, comfortable room, and you will begin to know the delight of feeling more stable and secure for a while. Always remember, however, that the spiral staircases of relationships have many levels to navigate, and some are steeper than others. Take it one step at a time. Easy does it.

CHAPTER 5

Step Three:
The Continuation Stage

At this point, you have been with the same partner for a little while. It could be a couple weeks or even several months, but either way, you've been together long enough for the relationship to feel smooth, stable, and promising. You should know, by now, if your communication styles are compatible and how to work through little snags when they come up. You and your lover have talked about relationship desires, needs, and goals, and after spending some quality time getting to know each other, you now know that you want to keep going. Together, you decide it's worth the love and effort it will take to be in a committed relationship. "Continuation" in a committed relationship doesn't necessarily mean marriage, however, or even exclusivity. This is where honest communication is absolutely in both of your best interests. Remember, this stage follows a mutual commitment to a long-term friendship, romantic relationship, or marriage.

I'll be honest with you: At this point in the relationship, it becomes difficult for someone to give specific advice, because every relationship is so different! The best thing you can do is continue practicing the good habits of self-awareness, authenticity, and good listening that you've been using in the earlier stages. Trust me, you still need all of them.

Relationships are wonderful, empowering, and create incredible amounts of happiness in our lives, but if you're not careful, it's easy to get stuck in ruts. Everything can be going along just splendidly, until one day you wake up and realize that you're bored, disconnected, or that your personal happiness is too tangled up in the relationship. There are many good ways to avoid this kind of relationship burnout, but all of them require regular, honest self-assessment. Are you still spending time on your own interests, or do you spend every moment of free time with (or thinking about) your significant other? Are you still building and nurturing other friendships? If you're in the habit of writing down your goals, glance back at a list of goals from before you started the relationship--are you making progress on any of them? Are you doing things that you know make you happy, even if they don't always involve your significant other?

If your answer to these questions is "no," then it might be time to readjust some of your priorities. If you find yourself falling into the same old "safe" sexual patterns, spend some intentional time thinking and searching out what it is you really want to experience sexually. Talk to your partner about it. Practice asking for what you want and be open to receiving those wants and needs from your partner. Focus on being emotionally present. It's also very important that you continue doing things that inspire and nourish you. It will make you a happier person and a more interesting lover, too!

The continuation stage can last any amount of time, from a few months to a whole lifetime, and this is where the real opportunities for personal, sexual, and romantic exploration appear. As someone who turned her life around by becoming a dominatrix, I would be remiss if I didn't talk at least a little bit about BDSM as a fun and exciting way to keep things interesting in the bedroom and to continue building trust.

A great way to get started with BDSM (just dipping a toe in the water, as it were) is to try out some fun, sexy role-playing. Having role-playing sexual fantasies is a normal, healthy curiosity. Even better, when we share and play out our desires with our partner, we become closer and more intimate through trust, which leads to a more loving relationship. Role-playing is a creative and sexy way to spice up regular intimacy.

If you want to try it out, start by talking about your fantasies with your partner. Good communication is essential if both of you are going to have a good time. (Are you noticing a theme here?) Tell your partner about things you're curious about and things you might want to try, and ask them about their fantasies too. Then go shopping together at the local sex store or online to pick out a few toys or sexy outfits to fulfill the role-play fantasy. Keep an open mind, start slow, and have fun!

Another good way to keep your relationship dynamic and exciting is to remember that the steamiest seduction begins long before you lay a hand on your partner. Send your partner spicy little texts throughout the day, talking about how and what you are going to do to each other once you get home. Once your partner is in your mind, sexually, your body will follow soon after, and so will theirs. So, gentlemen, and ladies, start your engines!

No matter how you decide to keep the fire burning between you and your partner, remember that exploring your sexuality is a lifelong process that begins and ends with you. One of the most important things we can learn is the almost unimaginable variety that can happen in our sexuality and the sexuality of others. Likes, dislikes, turn-ons and offs, wants, needs and desires can be exceedingly different from one person to the next, and our desires usually change and develop as we do.

It's incredibly freeing and empowering to truly experience, express, develop, and embrace our sexuality without judgment, whether we're working on it by ourselves or with a trustworthy, loving partner. In fact, it's healing. So, I challenge you and your partner to ask yourself the same questions I did when I first started exploring new forms of sexuality as a dominatrix— Can you be authentic about what you feel and desire even if others may not understand you right away? Can you let go of assumptions, judgments, and fears about how other people express their sexuality and instead learn from others with an open mind? I can promise from experience that if you decide to answer "yes" to both of these questions, you will experience freedom, personal growth, and healing like you've never felt before. Let your curiosity be your sex education teacher, and you will learn more than you ever thought possible.

With all this talk about steamy sex, it might be easy to forget that during the continuation stage, real life and rough spots can still happen. Sometimes, you and your partner will have misunderstandings, feelings will be hurt, and you will fight. This does not necessarily mean that your relationship is headed for the deterioration and termination stages, but it does mean that in those tense moments, some extra care, caution, and attention are essential.

Think of conflict as an aspect of positive development in your relationship(s). Really, I mean it. In the first place it shows that you are both having an influence on each other. And besides, when your lives are intertwined it's impossible not to have conflicting views from time to time, right?

In reality, it's not so much the reason for the conflict, but the manner in which you and your partner conduct yourselves that truly matters. Do you stay on topic, or do you "hit below the belt"? It's been said we show our character when we're in a fight, and I believe it's true. There's never a need to name-call, control our partner by physical force, or attack our partner's personality. Being straightforward, honest, and vulnerable goes a long way toward making sure that you talk about the problems rather than the person. Imagine how beautifully you can work out a conflict when you are open-minded, when you accept each other's opposing views, when you do your best not to take conflict too personally, and when you are willing to develop and transform.

To that end, when you argue with your partner, don't expect them to read your mind. If you're not sure what they're feeling, chances are good that they don't know what you feel either. It's completely unreasonable for either one of you to know that the other person is unhappy or unfulfilled in the relationship without self-expression and disclosure.

Additionally, it helps to be aware of the topics that tend to generate the most conflict. Research conducted by Siegert & Stamp (1994) assessed what provokes the typical couple's "First Big Fight" and the resulting consequences for their relationship. The four primary reasons for the "FBF" are:

1. Uncertainty about the commitment

2. Jealousy

3. Violation of relationship expectation

4. Personality and background differences

Looking at these four reasons for the FBF tells us that, before we ever enter a relationship, we need to have a pretty solid idea of who we are and what we want if we ever want to express ourselves well enough to really resolve conflicts in a mutually satisfying way. One of the most important ways to avoid having your relationship crippled by one of these four conflict areas is to never hold onto resentment. If you do, you'll be walking around like a pressure cooker, building up steam until you finally let it all out in an ugly and destructive explosion! Instead, let frustrations out slowly and consciously. Be selective about when, where, and how you decide to sort through and share your inner thoughts. Sifting through them in private first is your best bet. Think long and hard beforehand to identify exactly what the conflict is about before you jump into the fray. Make certain you're ready to have an open and honest discussion without lashing out from hurt or anger, and remember to be considerate and realistic.

Once you start the conversation, try to keep things in perspective, and try not to be too defensive. Stay positive, even when you and your partner seem to be disagreeing about vulnerable topics. One positive outcome is that when we're passionate about our thoughts and feelings and verbally express them, we raise our vibration, and when we fight with respect for our partner, good things can happen. You know exactly what I mean--being in a higher state of energy makes it easy to jump right into sexual vibrations for some hot and heavy fun! Woo-hoo!

Now that we've talked about how to fight fairly and with respect, here are a few final tips for developing and maintaining healthy communication for a happy, loving, and stable relationship.

Good Verbal Communication Habits

First and foremost, you need to be happy! When you're happy, you're sending out happy thoughts and feelings. Who the hell wants to be around a puss face? (If you feel like you'd need to fake it to come across as happy, skip ahead now to the section on Deterioration and Termination. You deserve to be happy, and if your current relationship makes that a strain, then it might be time to start making new, self-empowering choices.)

Have fun flirting, telling jokes, and especially be sure to include some pillow talk. Notice the words, phrases, and idiosyncrasies that your partner uses frequently, and use them to let your partner know that they are heard and appreciated. Talk about the future together, and trust your partner with the knowledge of your dreams, hopes, and fears. Tell your lover out loud that you love and appreciate them, and be specific about your favorite things about them. This can feel awkward at first, but whose heart wouldn't melt if their partner told them, "I love the way you smile at me--it makes me feel like the most important person in the world" or "You have an incredible singing voice, and I love it when you harmonize with me." If you want to do something really powerful, write your partner a letter that details your favorite things about them and your relationship, and read it out loud to them. You'll be amazed at how intimate the experience ends up being.

Once we're in a relationship, it can be easy to slip into just "I love you," which is still very meaningful, but it's also good to point out the little things you appreciate, admire, and love about your partner. This will really re-energize your love and make sure that both of you feel valued by the other on a daily basis.

Celebrate together by writing notes for birthdays or special occasions, sing together, and tell each other stories. During the day, touch base with your partner. Call just to say "I love you" or that they were on your mind. Plan adventures together. Just because you're both strong, independent people doesn't mean that you should miss out on the fun of putting together a trip or making a plan to explore a new place (DeVito, 2003). Above all, let your partner know that you're there for them, that you care, and that you always want the best from them. When in doubt, reassure them. It's so comforting to know that our partner appreciates us, and real expressions of love are always worth voicing.

Good NonVerbal Communication Habits

Maya Angelou said it best when she said, "The first time someone shows you who they are, believe them." I have made the dreaded mistake in the past of giving a man another chance (and another chance, and one more chance…) after I've already been disappointed. And sometimes, even after all those chances, I still end up giving him one more shot. Hey, what can I say? I'm optimistic.

Unfortunately, the times when I didn't trust my intuition and gave those second (and third and fourth) chances were the times I learned that I'd been right in the first place. In fact, 100% of the time the guy had literally shown me who he was, through his words and his actions, the very first time we met. I just hadn't wanted to believe it. In my experience, if a person is reliable, kind, and respectful, their personality will come across loud and clear in their actions at the very first meeting. (Of course don't forget that this goes both ways--your romantic interest will be watching to find out what kind of person you are, too, based on everything you communicate verbally and nonverbally.)

Was his car a garbage dump when he picked you up? Or maybe she forgot to show up for the first date altogether. Personally, either one would be a huge turn-off for me because those actions communicate, nonverbally, a lack of consideration and respect. I loved the example in the film The Bronx Tail when an older, more experienced gangster named Sonny LoSpecchio gives advice to a young, beautiful hottie named Calogero "C"

Anello about how to tell if a girl is sensitive or selfish—
in other words, a girl who makes it all about her:

> **Sonny:** *Alright, listen to me. You pull up right where she lives, right? Before you get outta the car, you lock both doors. Then, get outta the car, you walk over to her. You bring her over to the car. Dig out the key, put it in the lock and open the door for her. Then you let her get in. Then you close the door. Then you walk around the back of the car and look through the rear window. If she doesn't reach over and lift up that button so that you can get in: dump her.*
> **C:** *Just like that?*
> **Sonny:** *Listen to me, kid. If she doesn't reach over and lift up that button so that you can get in, that means she's a selfish broad and all you're seeing is the tip of the iceberg. You dump her and you dump her fast. (source: allsubs.org)*

It's often the comparatively simple things we do that demonstrate who we are, and much of this is communicated to the outside world through our body language, which means that in addition to listening with your ears, you need to learn to listen with your eyes as well. Did you know that 93% of the impact of the meaning of a message is revealed via nonverbal clues? (Leathers, 1997) For example, if your lover is explaining where he's been for the past two nights with a straight face but his foot is shaking back and forth, you can bet he's lying his ass off. Yeah, true! People figure that the way to counteract the lie is to keep emotion off their face, but because they are feeling a bit anxious—or turned on, or any other strong emotion—the energy has to be released somehow. And voilà. The foot swings or the fingers tap, most of the time an unconscious "tell." (Leathers, 1997). Awareness of what messages our bodies are communicating, then, is very important if we want to make a good, clear impression. If we like someone, we can tell them, but we can also find ways to express that liking with body language (Leathers, 1997). Some of the ways we can use our body to send a message include:

- Leaning forward during encounters (e.g., leaning across the dinner table to show interest in the person and conversation).

- Placing your body and head so that they are oriented to directly face the other person.

- Putting yourself in an "open-body" position (sitting with your arms crossed and your head down will not send an inviting message).

- Nodding your head affirmatively (making it obvious that you're listening).

- Gesturing in moderate amounts and being animated (the key word is *moderate*. Flailing your arms about and jumping up and down usually isn't a great way to make your conversational partner feel comfortable and heard).

- Maintaining a close interpersonal distance (without hovering).

- Making your body appear moderately relaxed (don't slouch, but don't be stiff as a board either).

- Touching (lean over and touch your partner on the arm or hand while they're talking).

- Initiating and *maintaining* eye contact (don't look away too quickly as if you felt it was a mistake in the first place).
- Smiling (always the best).

- Postural mirroring (e.g., mirroring their relaxed posture by relaxing yourself, which will give unspoken permission for both of you to relax).

I'm sure I don't need to explain that if you're not interested all you have to do is reverse the above body language. But if you're into expressing yourself on a positive note and your partner is expressing equal or more of the same, you're both on the right track to dopamine heaven!

CHAPTER **6**

Step Four:
Deterioration

At the end of the day, there's always the chance that you might decide that the bad outweighs the good in a relationship. There is no timeline for this kind of decision; it can happen on any "stair" of the relationship. To find out how you feel, try asking yourself: "How is this relationship affecting me?" and "Is this relationship bringing out the best in me, the not-so-great in me, or the worst in me?" Once again, entering any relationship with self-respect and self-love will serve you even when or if the relationship ends. The more empowered you are entering a relationship, the more self-assured you'll be exiting the relationship.

I started chatting online with "Mick" with a happy yellow face, but decided pretty early on that any relationship we tried to develop would reach the deterioration and termination stages pretty quickly. Every time we had a chat, he determinedly led the conversation in the direction of sex. On at least three occasions, I expressed how I felt: "Slow down, cowboy." When that didn't work, I decided on termination. The next time Mick opened a chat with me, I respectfully informed him that I didn't see our relationship going any further, and wished him good luck. He got back to me with, "We're not talking anymore? That sucks!" I found that pretty amusing, and responded by saying, "Honestly, I don't remember that we ever had a real conversation." Mick's finals words were "Okay, then..." I mean, really, I have a very full life, and if the only thing you can bring to the table is a hard-on, I'm going to keep moving. I can get that at home alone, and I don't even have to shave my legs!

CHAPTER 7

Step Four: Termination

I'm not trying to make light of the end of any relationship carries a great investment of time and emotion. However, if the relationship is not serving you, and you have exhausted the ways to work it out, it's time to move on to happiness.

> *"Grasping at things can only yield one of two results: Either the thing you are grasping at disappears, or you yourself disappear. It is only a matter of which occurs first."*
>
> —Goenka

This is why it's so important to be "whole" when you enter into relationships. And, by the way, that also means being financially independent. Getting stuck in a bad relationship due to lack of funds is a sure path to heartbreak. You need to be able to make all your decisions from self-love, self-respect, and self-worth. And it would really lend a hand if you came in with what David Steele calls "consciousness" in his book *Conscious Dating*. In it, Steele makes it crystal clear that we have real choices not only in the beginning of a relationship, but throughout every stage of romantic and sexual involvements to stay or to go our separate ways. Never make the mistake of staying in an unfulfilling relationship full of drama and unhappiness --while you're struggling to make things work, you could easily miss the greatest love of your life.

I definitely believe that we can all find our soul mates, the people who will be our lovers and our best friends, as long as we learn to truly be ourselves, practice communicating well, and don't settle. It's my philosophy that every human being deserves and can attain lives of happiness and love, and I hope that reading this book has given you encouragement and direction on your individual journey to find fulfillment. Always remember, you are valuable, you deserve love and happiness, and the most important part of being a good, committed loving partner is to be good, committed, and loving toward your true self first

References

Devito, Joseph A. (2003). *Human communication: The basic course.* Pearson, 182–223.

Levinger, G. (1983). *Development and change.* New York: W. H. Freeman and Company, 315–359.

Merriam-Webster. (n.d.) *"Acquaintance."* Retrieved from http://www.merriam-webster.com/dictionary/acquaintance

Allsubs.org. (n.d.) *Movie quotes for A Bronx Tale.* Retrieved from http://www.allsubs.org/search-movie-quotes/'a%20Bronx%20Tale'/

Siegert, J. R. & G. H. Stamp. (1994). *"Our first big fight"* as a milestone in the development of close relationships. Communication Monographs 61, 345–360.

Leathers, Dale G. (1997). *Successful nonverbal communication, principles and applications.* (3rd ed.). Pearson, 81, 255.

About the Author

Sandra is an author, speaker, and CEO/ Founder of Attainment Studios, a sex positive business directory website designed to bring together members of the sex-positive community, and for finding solutions for your professional and personal needs. She is an expert in communications, life transformation, authentic living, health, wellness, and intimacy.

Sandra is also an internationally featured Huffington Post blogger, a regular writer for Arianna Huffington's new health and wellness platform Thrive Global, and among the top 10% of writer on Medium in 2016. She was listed as having the "Coolest Job in NYC" by Thrillist NYC, and her interview and photo shoot with Huffington Post '15 Unbelievable Photos Of A 60-Year-Old Dominatrix With Her Client' article made the 'MOST SHARED', WHAT'S HOT and 'TRENDING' lists on The Huffington Post in the United States and Australia.

Her recent book *Switch: Time for a Change*, is a memoir about how her later profession as a dominatrix ultimately allowed her to change her previously blind adherence to "the rules," and to enter into a whole different kind of contract with a truer version of herself. Sandra was able to change her thoughts, feelings, and beliefs in order to embrace a passionate and fulfilled life.

LaMorgese holds degrees in communications, holistic nutrition, and metaphysical science, and she is practitioner certified in hypnotherapy, aromatherapy, colon hydrotherapy, muscle testing, acupuncture, ozone therapy, and licensed in cosmetology and esthetics.

Sandra is also a professionally trained actor who studied method, film, and television at the prestigious Lee Strasberg Theatre Institute, commercial acting at the School for Film & Television, and media presentation training at On Camera . . . and Off, Inc. with Larry Conroy, all in New York City.

info@sandralamorgese.com
http://sandralamorgese.com
http://www.huffingtonpost.com/sandra-lamorgese-phd
https://journal.thriveglobal.com/@lamorgeses
https://medium.com/@lamorgeses